How it all started.

When my one of my sons, Mike first car. I had no problem with that as he had a little money saved up but I started questioning his reasoning when he said he wanted a 1967 Impala 4 door hardtop. All I knew about these cars is that when I was growing up only your Grandparents drove them! After all, I grew up in the muscle car era and a 4 door was hardly considered a muscle car. And I wasn't just thinking muscle, I was thinking looks also. Come on, who in their right mind would put money into a 4 door?

Well since that day I have learned a lot! They are not easy to find, not easy to retrieve, not cheap or easy to fix up but the most important factor I learned along the way is the car (fixed up right) has a cult following (like none other) because of the TV show Supernatural. The Impala has a major role in the show and the fans just love it, and that is exactly why my son wanted it! So the hunt was on.

This book will assist those who are in the process or considering turning a 1967 Impala 4 door hardtop into a Supernatural car (aka Metallicar)!

First our story:

After many days of research and many, many more months hunting for this specific car we finally found one in Oregon (We live in TN). It was a 283 4 door HT (Hard Top) that needed work but hey, we found one!

This car was in fair shape. Had the typical surface rust, especially around the base of the vinyl top. It also had a very good frame and some holes in the floorboards and trunk. There was rust on some of the body panels. The 283 engine ran but was weak. Not a factory

A/C car and it was missing some molding. But because it came from out west it was a fairly rust free car.

Not too bad looking!

Area that needed repairs.

Driver's floor board had some minor holes. The rest was fine.

Seats were dry rotted.

So now what do we do? After buying the car we (he) didn't have much money left so we considered our options. I knew basic automotive skills and my son was willing to do whatever he could to get this looking like the car in the TV show. So he borrowed some money from his brothers to start working on the body.

First he took out the seats and all the carpet. We found some rust holes in the floorboards but not too bad. The door panels were in great shape. After considering buying all the sanding equipment to start the paint removal process, we decided to start removing the layers of paint with airplane paint remover. We thought it to be the cheaper route than sanding so we proceeded very carefully. We were told to be careful using this approach because if you leave any residue in the cracks it might come through the paint later.

Here's the car with the seats out.

Here you can see the start of the stripping process.

As you can see in the picture we left the molding and glass and hardware intact while doing this. (It all had to come off but I'll tell about that a little later).

So we worked on it whenever we had some free time. In taking the paint off we found spots of small body damage that was repaired throughout the years with Bondo. There wasn't much rust but it did have a lot of small nicks and dents. Since our car was a vinyl top we had to take all that off also. And when we removed the material we found some rust around the windows. Mostly surface rust, but it still had to be dealt with.

Also there are little metal pins that go around the base of the vinyl top where the molding attaches. All of that had to be ground off.

We worked on it and worked on it.

This is what it looked like during the paint removal.

The aircraft paint remover did a good job of getting through all the layers of paint. We just had to be careful using it. The stuff would burn you quickly if you got any of it on you! We put it on with small paint brushes and removed it with putty knives.

Another consideration is that you should remove all the Bondo that was previously on the body as the aircraft paint remover tends to soften up the Bondo. You want a fresh surface to prepare for paint.

We did find some new areas that needed repair once we got into the sanding. But still, nothing really bad or uncommon. That's why you always try and find a car that's in the best original shape you can. It saves so much work (and money) later. If it's original you can see what's wrong with it. You don't want to buy a car that someone has done a hack job on the repairs and then covered it up with paint or primer. Original is always better.

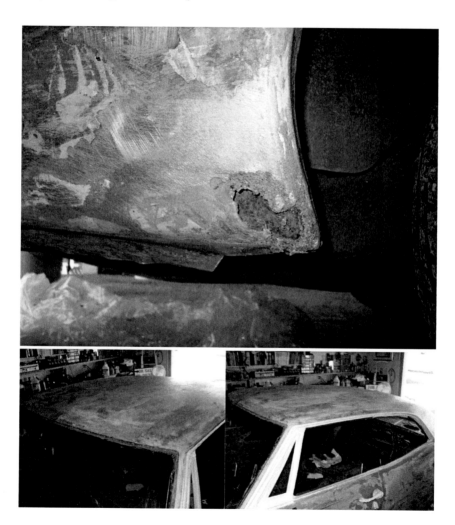

We took the front and back bumper off when we started the paint removal.

Now here comes the fun part. After we worked many hours on getting the paint off we had to decide how we were going to prep the body for paint. We researched the cost of buying all the prep equipment and material versus paying to have someone do it. After much debate we decided on searching for someone to do it as cheaply as we could get by with (bad mistake).

Because most modern auto repair shops like to deal strictly with insurance jobs we had a very hard time locating someone that could do the job for a reasonable price. Word of mouth led us to a semi-retired man with his own little garage shop in which he did all his work. He wasn't far from us so he looked at the car, gave us an unbelievable quote and said he could have it back to us quick including a paint job! Yes we hit the jackpot!

Here we are picking it up, didn't look bad for the money I thought.

But after bringing it home and looking at it REAL close, the paint job was missing paint in areas and bugs and sand were imbedded in the paint!

We immediately called the painter up and worked out a deal (because he didn't want to repaint it, and we didn't want him to) to just refund some of the money.

So now we had to start all over looking for a good place to get the body sanded and painted again!

All that mishap took place in the fall. It wasn't until winter was almost over when we started searching for body shops again. What we found out is that the only places that would consider doing the car were restoration shops. The reason we originally kept our distance from these shops was cost. They are usually very high end and expensive. But after contacting multiple shops we were able to come to an agreement with one where we would take all the hardware, chrome, and glass off the car and the restoration shop would prep and paint the car. We would have to put everything back together ourselves. That sounded like something we could do, so we were happy to get going again.

While the car was sitting in the garage during the winter we wanted to do something with the 283 engine. We thought about rebuilding it but I didn't think it was worth putting money into the 283 so we looked around for a better engine. Some time went by and we finally found a rebuilt 1968 327 engine in Kentucky that had been listed on a local internet site. We drove up there and bought the new, rebuilt 327 complete with a brand new Eldebrock carb for $1000. The engine had all high end internal components and the owner said it was pushing 350hp. Perfect! Now we had a vital part of our Supernatural car and we were heading home with it. (Although we got a great deal on the engine and it helped keep costs down, if I hadn't found this one online we were planning on getting the engine from Jegs or Summit as they both have great customer service if we ever needed anything).

Over the next couple of weeks we pulled the 283 out and replaced it with the 327. (While the engine was out we also pulled the radiator and gas tank and had them cleaned and repaired where needed). It was not too complicated of a job and working together we had it in and running in short order. (If you are doing this for your first time, take plenty of pictures for reference). We made sure to run special engine break in oil that has zinc in it. It was highly recommended from an engine rebuilder.

When it was time to take the car to the body shop again we had the interior out, glass out, bumpers off, all trim and hardware off.

The body shop worked weeks on getting the body sanded down and straight. After many hours of sanding it was ready for paint. The black paint went on. We used Dupont Nason 2010 Chevy truck black. We also had the body shop paint the dash and door panels tan as in the show.

The exact color is *SEM #15093 Light Buckskin.*

While we were in the middle of the restoration my son contacted the Supernatural convention that was going to be held in Nashville and they said if it was completed in time they would love to have it at their convention. No pressure here I thought, we only have to get the car home and completely put it back together, all by ourselves! After the car was painted we had less than a month to put it all back together. The body shop (knowing what was in store for us) didn't think we could make the time limit and they told us so.

So I took a few days off work and we began putting it back together. First we put in the new carpet. (The carpet in the show is gold but we went with black carpet as a nice contrast.)

Then we put the refurbished seats in. Then we started on the molding and hardware. All the side glass had to be put back and then the door panels attached. We had an auto glass company install a new windshield and reinstall the rear glass for us. We took off the front drum brakes and installed disk brakes.

We installed headers on the engine. Then we took the car to a local muffler shop and had a new exhaust system installed.

Next, we put on the correct tires and wheels.

We found the correct center caps online.

Whenever my son had any down time he was researching (or making) items for the trunk's weapons cache. Now that really took a lot of time, I'll expound more on that later.

Once we got the car pretty much put back together we worked on making the weapons cache box for the trunk. We used dimensions that we obtained on our own by looking at stop action TV video footage from the show. We messed up a time or two but finally came up with something that looked right. Maybe not perfect but close.

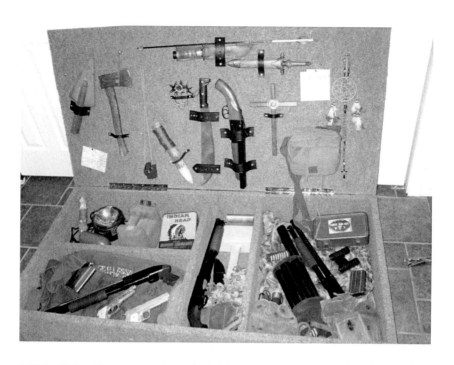

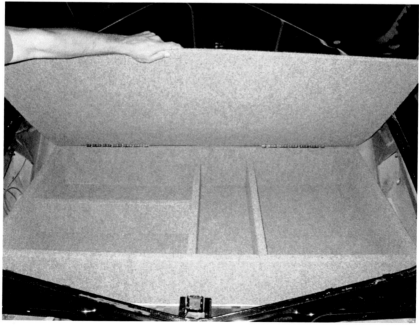

Well what do you think?

One of the last things to put on the car was the bumper guards. These are very hard to find because they don't make reproductions of these as with the side molding and back glass etc...

Front Bumper Guards

Rear Bumper Guards

We made it to the convention with just a couple of days to spare. The only thing we didn't have time to do was replacing the headliner which has since been installed. The paint shop painted it tan before the installation.

The whole cast was able to autograph the car for us!

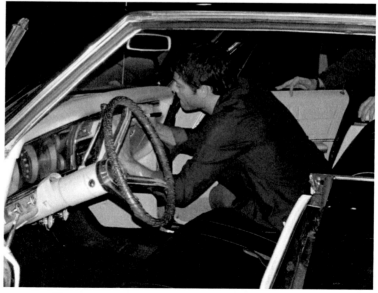

There were some very happy fans that day!

This is what the finished product looked like!

Was it worth it? Yes!

Now, what we have learned.

When looking for a 1967 Impala 4 door hardtop to restore, make sure it's an Impala hardtop! People are selling 4 door Caprice's and claiming they are Supernatural cars. They are not. They don't have the right interior nor do they have the proper molding.

And speaking of molding, try to find a car with all the side and rear molding intact. They don't (as of yet) make reproduction molding for the 4 door hardtops. The front end clip is the same as on any

1967 Impala so all that is available on the reproduction aftermarket. But from the front clip back, you're on your own. (I have heard that the molding on a Impala 4 door pillar car might work but I have never had one to compare so do your own research on that one).

The actual show car has factory A/C, it is a big plus if you can find one. There weren't as many made with the factory air so they are the rarest of all the Impala 4 dr hardtops, you are very lucky if you can snag one!

Do not try to convert a post car either it'll be a waste of money. True fans know the difference and if you ever need to sell it you most likely won't get your investment back.

You can get aftermarket front windshield glass but they don't make the rear aftermarket glass so make sure the rear glass is OK on the car you buy (and make sure whoever is doing the body work takes care when removing and storing the rear glass).

The same goes with the side glass. Your best bet if you need any replacement parts is to look online or search for a parts car.

Interior door panels are very important also. They have started to make replacement panels but they are not of the same quality as the originals and are missing the "buttons". So if your car has good panels it's a definite plus.

Also try to find cars that have the corner lights on them. Correct Supernatural cars need them. You can find corners light on the internet but make sure to get the attaching brackets with them as most don't seem to come with them and you'll need them to attach the lights to the body.

The rear trunk molding is a very elusive piece if you have to search for it. As this molding can only come from another 4 door hardtop or convertible. It is a very hard piece to find anywhere so having a good one on your car to begin with is a great big plus!

Most gas tanks will have to be taken off to be cleaned and re lined.

We also installed air shocks to compensate for the extra weight the weapons cache added to the trunk.

Front and rear bumper guards are needed as well. These can get pricey but do come up on the internet every so often. So if your car has them to begin with that's another bonus. They do not make reproduction 1967 Impala bumper guards.

Also when you are buying the wheels, have them balanced as soon as you can. We let ours sit while the body work was being done and when we went to put the tires on them they were warped from the factory and couldn't be balanced! It's easier to talk to the factory representative when the wheels haven't been sitting for half a year!

Tire sizes:

The front tires are BF Goodrich p215/70r15 on a 15x7 wheel.

The rear tires are BF Goodrich p275/60/r15 on 15x8 wheels.

Wheel size:

Front (Cragar 330 Super Spoke) 15"x7", bolt circle 5" x 4-3/4" Rear spacing 4-1/2"

Rear (Cragar 330 Super Spoke) 15"x8", bolt circle 5" x 4-3/4" Rear spacing 4-3/4"

I would recommend that the front brakes be upgraded to disk, especially if you upgrade the engine. Either way front disk brakes are the way to go.

Also remember the car emblems are removed on the TV show so you will want to fill those holes in when prepping for the paint.

We also had the tranny rebuilt, just in case.

As you disassemble your car take plenty of pictures or videos because there usually is a long period before you put the parts back on and what you thought you could remember you can't!

Everyone's costs on building a Supernatural car will vary depending on how much you paid for the car originally, condition of the car, extent you want to restore it, and of course how much work you do yourself. But if I had to give an estimate on how much it would cost to get an average condition car looking like a Supernatural car (not ground up restoration and excluding the weapons cache) I would say approximately $15,000-$18,000. And that's above what you paid for the car!

One of the reasons these cars are hard to find to begin with is that in the past they were never really collectable and when scrap metal prices rose, anyone that had one laying around scraped it. Although Chevrolet made over 500,000 series 64 cars, they didn't keep any records on how many of them were 4 door hard tops. So to the best of my knowledge no one knows exactly how many were ever made. And no one knows how many there are left either! On a recent Ebay auction I was watching last week a 1967 Impala 4 door hardtop went up for sale. It was a very low mileage car that had a 6 cylinder engine without factory air. The car was in beautiful condition. It sold for $16,900 not counting any other fees. So these cars are increasing in value fast. The interest in this car is not just from fans here in the USA, it has exploded overseas as the show's increasing popularity has spread to every continent. So in my opinion these cars are a great investment.

Some 1967 Impala 4 door pictures for reference. (283 engine)

(396 engine) Only one I have ever seen in a 4 door hardtop!

What a factory air dash looks like.

A few nice 4 door Impalas.

Nice original car.

283's & 327's are almost identical. Most 327's have 4 barrels.

Paperwork such as the Protecto plate would be an added plus. But not so much if you are putting a new engine in as the Protecto plate matches the engine ID to the car ID. It's still nice to have any history that goes with the car.

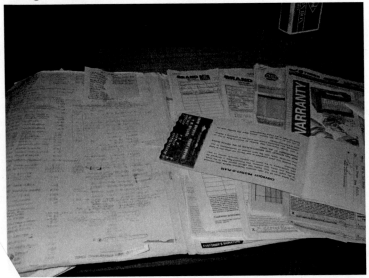

Here are trunk floor panels that are in good original condition.

Here is a survivor car with very low mileage.

Some pictures just for fun!

Pictured left to right, our friend Hem and my son Mike with their Impalas. Hem drove from California to see Mike!

Hem bought a car from us and had it restored. It came out beautiful and he loves it to death!

Mike was invited to a SHOWCON convention in Nashville!

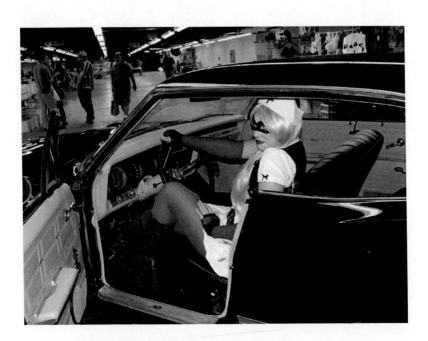

Everyone loved the car!

It was a tough day for Mike.

Mike's car "Hunter," completely finished.

The weapons cache

My son made most of the items in the weapons cache. Hard to find items would be the 1 gallon Indian Head hydraulic fluid oil can in decent shape. The airsoft guns are sometimes hard to find as they stopped making some of them. The 1836 Colt Patterson was found as a kit and my son hand painted it. The dagger was and still is the hardest item to find.

What we have in our weapons cache:

Custom made wooden arrow spear, axe, map, compass, ninja throwing stars, machete, mad max metal and wood double barrel shotgun (airsoft), custom made wooden cross, KA-BAR style knife with leather sheath, carbon arrow with broad head, Supernatural news article, military drum mag pouch, 2x brass knuckle paperweights, dream catcher, rosary beads, Ithaca M37 Airsoft shotgun, 1911 Airsoft pistol, Taurus 92 Airsoft pistol, Airsoft pump shotgun, The "Colt" pistol, custom made grenade launcher w/shell, wooden mallet/hammer, two flasks, Indian Head oil can, small gas tank, spotlight, several wooden spikes, beil axe, military bags, wooden sheath dagger, medic gear. (Note) In the picture we have a real 870 Express pump shotgun for looks. It doesn't stay with the other items!

Our dimensions were 57 inches by 29 inches. Depth was 7 ½ inches with the interior partitions being 5-¾ inches deep. We just used grey indoor/outdoor carpet to cover it.

Weapons Cache plans measured in inches

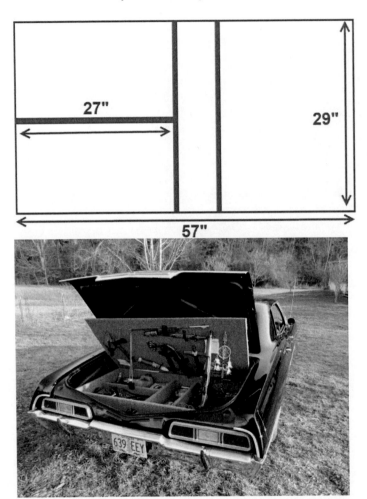

There is a certain type of material that was used in the show. We tried to find it but never could. So we went with the carpet. Now it should really be a little more dirty and darkened up some to match the show more closely but hey!

I believe Mike was happy with the finished product!

I wish well to all those that are searching for the perfect 1967 Chevy Impala 4 door hardtop to turn into their own Metallicar, (aka Baby) the '67 Impala in the TV show Supernatural. It took us a long time to find and complete Mike's car. It was tough chasing down parts and making deals where needed. We've met a lot of people and made a bunch of new friends. We've learned a lot and we've spent a lot. But there is nothing that can beat rolling around the corner of some car show and hear the scream of a fan that just spotted "Baby!"

Made in the USA
San Bernardino, CA
25 March 2015